YOUR KNOWLEDGE HAS VALUE

- We will publish your bachelor's and
  master's thesis, essays and papers

- Your own eBook and book -
  sold worldwide in all relevant shops

- Earn money with each sale

Upload your text at www.GRIN.com
and publish for free

Jan Kussowski

Aus der Reihe: e-fellows.net stipendiaten-wissen

e-fellows.net (Hrsg.)

Band 1192

Risk Management within the IT-Service Lifecycle

GRIN Publishing

Bibliographic information published by the German National Library:

The German National Library lists this publication in the National Bibliography; detailed bibliographic data are available on the Internet at http://dnb.dnb.de .

Imprint:

Copyright © 2014 GRIN Verlag GmbH
Print and binding: Books on Demand GmbH, Norderstedt Germany
ISBN: 978-3-656-96103-1

This book at GRIN:

http://www.grin.com/en/e-book/299681/risk-management-within-the-it-service-lifecycle

GRIN - Your knowledge has value

Since its foundation in 1998, GRIN has specialized in publishing academic texts by students, college teachers and other academics as e-book and printed book. The website www.grin.com is an ideal platform for presenting term papers, final papers, scientific essays, dissertations and specialist books.

Risk Management within the

IT-Service Lifecycle

Bachelor Thesis

Lehrstuhl für Wirtschaftsinformatik,

FH Brandenburg University of applied sciences
Brandenburg an der Havel

von
Jan Kussowski

Wirtschaftsinformatik
9. Fachsemester

Table of Contents

List of Figures

List of Tables

List of Abbreviations

BISII   Business IT Strategic Investment Index
BRM   Business Relationship Management
BVIS   Business Value Index for Services
CI   Configuration Item
CIM   Computer Integrated Manufacturing
CSI   Continual Service Improvement
GxP   Good (Laboratory, Clinical, Manufacturing) Practices
IRM   Institute for Risk Management
ISACA   Information Systems Audit and Control Associations
IS   Information Services
ISO   International Organization for Standardization
IT   Information Technology
ITIL   Information Technology Infrastructure Library
ITSC   IT-Service Component
KPI   Key Performance Indicator
MGMT   Management
OGC   Office of Government Commerce
OLA   Operational Level Agreement
PaaS   Platform as a Service
PLM   Product Lifecycle Management
PO   Process Owner
RFC   Request for Change
RM   Risk Manager
RSM   Relationship Manager
SaaS   Software as a Service
SDM   Service Delivery Manager
SLA   Service Level Agreement
SM   Service Management
SO   Service Owner
SOA   Service Oriented Architecture
SOP   Standard Operation Procedure
SPM   Service Portfolio Manager

Abstract

Risk Management for IT-Service Lifecycle Management is not always performed in a transparent, repeatable and consistent way. In consequence its potential to be used as a key element for successful decision taking is not fully utilized.

This thesis considers applied standards, models and practices in the IT-Service Management to establish a methodology which enables improvement of Risk Management within the IT-Service Lifecycle. The developed methodology determines stages in the Lifecycle where risk assessments should be performed. It also defines the required information and their sources.

Being based on already existing processes within a service providing organization, this methodology can easily be applied to improve the service quality.

Keywords: Risk Management, IT-Services, Service Lifecycle

Motivation

Since one major business sector of Merck is the production of pharmaceutical products the organization is subject to very strict regulations for development and production of their life science products and the business supporting IT-Services therefore underlie a strong IT-Governance. This IT-Governance as part of the corporate Governance is highly influential on how IT-Services are operated and carried out over their whole lifecycle. In addition, business processes and the management of risks are highly important factors. The provided IT-Services have to be on track with business needs of the respective customers. To ensure this alignment strategic decisions need to be based on relevant information. To improve this decision making process various types of information on IT-Services are needed.

The author's professional background served as a foundation for addressing this corporate need of Merck. Having obtained basic knowledge on IT-Services, related organizations and processes, the author took this opportunity to pursue his growing interest within this field of research.

1   Introduction

Risk Management is an important tool to steer and improve IT-Service operations during their lifecycle. This provides an advantage to the service provider as well as the customer. Risk Management already plays an important part in various types of business Key Performance Indicators. For IT-Services which are implemented through a Lifecycle process, an initial risk assessment is carried out, but changes of the risk level within the Lifecycle are very often not measured and addressed.

If the risks during the Lifecycle are recognized, addressed and treated appropriately, the IT-Service management itself and the IT-organization as a whole is able to increase its daily performance and their progress towards strategic goals.

This thesis provides a methodology for integrating Risk Management in the IT-Service Lifecycle allowing risk based decisions regarding service quality. This is applicable during the whole Lifecycle from project initiation through service provisioning until service decommissioning.

Service providing organizations need to know which risks for the customer and for the providing organization could result from the services they offer. Based on the identification and assessment of these risks the organization is able to decide if and in which way it wants to take action. Risk Management should be beneficial for the assessments of services.

To address this topic, various concepts and standards are taken into account. First, process activities, roles and strategic influences on the Service Lifecycle are described. ITIL and industry related standards are taken into account and compared to currently applied processes at Merck's Information Services department.

To gain an overview on the existing and relevant Risk Management standards, ISO 31000 and the ISACAs (Information Systems Audit and Control Association) approach are analyzed. This includes Risk Management principles, the Risk Management process and the Risk Management framework.

Important risks during the IT-Service Lifecycle are identified. The relevant risk priorities are determined by KPIs, CSFs as well as Input and Output of applicable ITIL processes at Merck. Additionally, legal and regulatory requirements which Merck is subject to are taken into account. These priorities are then analyzed to point out which of them are important and when they should be reviewed.

Based on the risks previously determined certain points within the Lifecycle are chosen at which applicable priorities are reviewed for each IT-Service. Further recommendations for risk identification, assessment and treatment are presented. As several risks will be assessed throughout the lifecycle a portfolio visualization for the most important risks are chosen. This gives additional possibilities in cases of comparison and evaluation of their potential impact. This provides respective service owners useful assistance for making risk-based decisions on their IT-Service.

By reading this thesis the reader is able to obtain an introduction to Service lifecycle principles and ITIL concepts and processes, as well as Risk Management procedures based on ISO 31000. For this Thesis only practical procedures and concepts are taken into account which fit the need of Merck's Information Services department. The identified risks and created methods aim to give an extended view on how risks can be assessed and treated in an IT-Service providing environment. This thesis aims to achieve an applicable Risk Management method which serves the business requirements for Merck's IT-Service department.

2 The Service Lifecycle

When addressing the IT-Service Lifecycle it is important to know the origin of lifecycle models and concepts. In the past manufactured goods went through a production cycle. As soon as IT was developed the way goods were produced drastically changed.

While the diversification over various economic sectors took place, the perception for IT-products changed accordingly. In a society mostly characterized by the service business sector this also applies to the production of Information Technology as the combination of hardware, software and business processes.

2.1 Lifecycle concepts

The Lifecycle concept which attempts to describe the lifespan of a product in various stages has its origin in the industrial production (Porter, 1980). Products run through a Lifecycle which can be divided in the phases Introduction, Growth, Maturity and Decline (Matys, 2013).

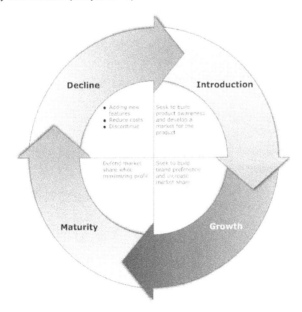

Figure 1 product Lifecycle based on (Matys, 2013).

As the products and processes of a company evolve over the time, the supporting IT-Services have to change similarly to maintain the level of business support. Therefore the changes within the Lifecycle need to be addressed by the responsible for this product in form of management actions. With the development of Computer Integrated Manufacturing (CIM) in the beginning of 80s, the attempt to steer industrial production processes with Information Technology was commencing (Bullinger et al., 2006). Since then the production of goods is getting increasingly complex over the years which created the need for appropriate management tools to support the product Lifecycle in each phase. For IT-products e.g. Software, these phases introduced by (Matys, 2013) can be translated into Plan, Build, Run, and Retirement of the Software based on (Zarnekow et al., 2003).

According to (Bullinger et al., 2006) this Product Lifecycle Management (PLM) is a concept to effectively manage products throughout the whole cycle. This need of product management can easily be transferred to the production of IT-Services. Throughout the years as standards and reference models were developed (e.g. Information Technology Infrastructure Library), the way IT-Service products are seen has gone through a drastically change. Originating from Software Development and Engineering the Service Oriented Architecture (SOA) has gradually taken over and changed how IT-Products are planned, build, run and decommissioned. IT allows customers to use solutions in parts or as a whole on a pay-per-use basis (Software as a Service, Platform as a Service) (Fischbach et al., 2013).

(Zarnekow et al., 2003) addressed this change as Integrated Information Management which serves as a methodology for a product oriented Information Management. Their model states the change towards a Source, Make and Deliver process for IT-products which need to be tailored to the customer's needs (Zarnekow and Brenner, 2003).

Figure 2 Value chain of IS organizations and IT resource management based on (Erek, 2012)

As shown in figure 2 the Lifecycle element describes the ongoing influence of strategy and the systems on which the service production process is based. Relationships between service provider and customer become increasingly important since business needs and the procurement of internal or external products have to be aligned to offer the best possible support in order to reach the strategic goals. Therefore this connection between IT and business can be described as a socket which enables businesses to be more effective and efficient (Woitsch et al., 2009).

The fundamental concepts that permit the integration of the basic IT components into a single logically consistent model of the corporate information system include business service, IT service, and service Lifecycle. The concepts of service and its Lifecycle permit satisfactory representation of the operation of the corporate information system as a logical sequence of processes and functions and provide the basis of the effective solution of many pressing IT problems.(Zimin and Kulakov, 2010)

2.2 ITIL Service Lifecycle

Within the previous chapter the concept of the Lifecycle was introduced to clarify the origin of IT-Service production principles. Over the years the "common practice model" ITIL rose to an often referred principle for standardization and suggested management tool for complex IT-Infrastructures. The main goal of ITIL is to implement an IT-Service management with standardized processes and activities. Key factor of this whole reference model is the alignment between the customer (e.g. operational business) and the service providing institution (e.g. internal IT-departments or external IT-provider) (OGC, 2011c).

A service is defined as:

"A means of delivering value to customers by facilitating outcomes customers want to achieve without the ownership of specific costs and risks." (OGC, 2011c).

Within ITIL the Service Lifecycle is described as process for the IT-Service Management and is defined by 5 different Phases:

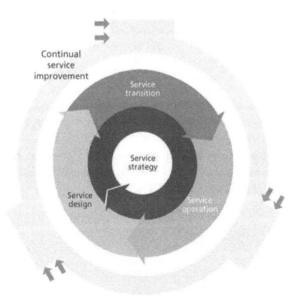

Figure 3 Service Lifecycle according to ITIL (Beims, 2012, OGC, 2011c)

The introduced model describes 5 phases, each suggesting different processes and activities which can lead to a more efficient operation of the IT, deliver a better service quality to the respective customers and increase the customer satisfaction while reducing costs.

Service Strategy

- Serves as a starting point for all activities during the Service Lifecycle and offers support and guidance for service design, development and implementation.
- Securing Alignment of Business and IT-Services.
- Defines strategic aims and identifies chances and possibilities for new IT-Services.
- Reflects on costs and risks of the service portfolio.

Service Design

- Implements the presets that were defined within Service Strategy and delivers Templates for the conception of adequate and innovative IT-Services.
- Designing of new and altered services are taken into consideration as well as service management processes.
- Topics covered are the service catalogue, capacity, continuity and service level management.

Service Transition

- Delivers a guidance and process elements for the transition into to the business environment
- Addresses Topics such as Changes within the business culture, knowledge- and Risk Management

Service Operation

- Focusses on daily business of the service operation.
- Addresses the effective and efficient delivery and support of services, which aims to generate a value for the customer and the service provider.
- Includes processes such as Incident or problem management as well as application management and technical management for measurement and controlling of functions and processes.

Continual Service Improvement (CSI)

- Basic support and guidance for value generation and conservation for the customer through continuously improving Service Design, Service Transition and Operation.
- Methods for Quality management, Change Management and Capability Improvement are combined.

Figure 4 shows relevant ITIL processes which carry out the activities described within the 5 phases of the IT-Service Lifecycle.

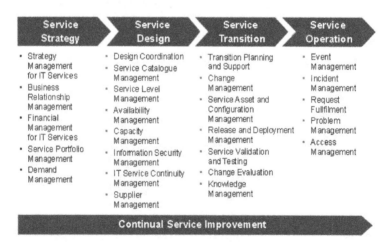

Figure 4 process overview for ITIL Service Lifecycle derived from (OGC, 2011c)

Roles and activities

ITIL defines various roles which aim to assist the above mentioned processes and actives during the Lifecycle.

Service Owner

- Aims to preserve the accordance of services and customer requests.
- Identifies and realizes means to improve the services.
- Gathers all relevant information for effective service Monitoring.
- Guarantees Service Level Agreement (SLA) compliant Service Performance.

Process Owner

- Documents and reviews the processes
- Defines Key Performance Indicators for measuring of efficiency and effectiveness of the process.
- Designs and continually improves the process, including constant review of roles, responsible personnel, KPIs and documentation.

2.3 Merck IT-Service Lifecycle

Since Merck is currently in the process of changing and reorganizing their Information Service department, the implementation and improvement of ITIL methods and process is an ongoing project.

As described in chapter 2.1 the strategic alignment between IT-Services and business processes is a crucial part of economic growth for Merck. Key factors which influence the decision on adding new services to the portfolio are the business strategy and business capability which are directly reflected by the IT Strategy.

The IT-Service Lifecycle, its processes and activities are managed by the service owners, who are responsible to actively influence the Service Lifecycle (including new, changed and retired services) by maximizing generated business value by the IT department.

IT-Service Lifecycle Overview

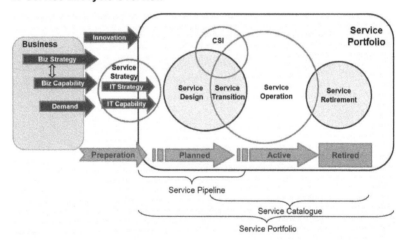

Figure 5 Merck IT-Service process overview (Merck 2012)

As Figure 5 illustrates, the IT-Service process at Merck originates from ITIL process concepts and terminology. Additionally Merck applied checkpoints within their processes which imply the status in which the IT-Service currently resides.

Merck Process Status	ITIL Phase
Preparation	Service Strategy
Planned	Service Design, Service Transition
Active	Service Operation
Retired	Included in ITIL Service Operation

Table 1 Merck service portfolio status in comparison to ITIL Lifecycle Phases

The Service Strategy phase serves as the initiation point at which business demand and value of the proposed IT-Service is determined. As described in the IT-Service Lifecycle according to ITIL, key activities according to chapter 2.2 apply. The service owner (SO) is responsible to verify his service Portfolio against the current need of the business based on the strategic aspects and to fulfill the future business needs and innovations. When business requirements are identified, a new draft for a service demand is created. In order to align Business needs and IT capability strategy of business and IT are to be assessed and verified regularly. To assist the decision which services should be operated to support business demand, Merck uses a Business Value Index for Services (BVIS)

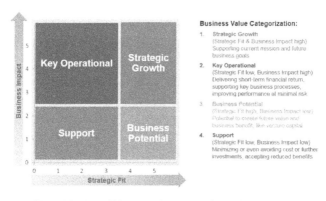

Figure 6 Business Value Index for Services (BVIS) (Merck 2012)

Merck uses this methodology to measure value of the business IT-Services. This helps to evaluate the current strategic position of the respective business IT-Service within the service portfolio. It helps to determine if a service is critical for business success or whether it may be discontinued. The services which are currently supported by the Information Services Department should aim towards a strategic growth, therefore current and future strategic objectives should be supported. If services don't support strategic objectives they pose a risk to the service providing department (IS) as well as for the operational business itself. Aims for cost efficient service delivery and business value won't be achieved. Future investing in services that don't support strategic goals should be reduced to a minimum or the service itself should be exchanged or discontinued.

In the forthcoming chapters this methodology will assist linking risk scenarios to business value to determine the risk tolerance. Merck therefore has adapted a process modell which includes activities defined by the PDCA or Deming Cycle (Deming, 1986) to serve the service portfolio activities included in the service Lifecycle processes.

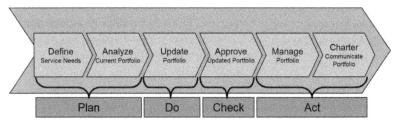

Figure 7 Service Lifecycle activities (Merck 2012)

The Plan-Do-Check-Act methodology should focus on the most important aspects for service management (ISO, 2012):

- Understanding and fulfilling the service requirements and achieve customer satisfaction
- Establishing the policy and objectives for the processes
- Designing and delivering services that add value to the customer
- Monitoring, measuring and reviewing performance of services within the service portfolio
- Continually improving the services on objective measurements

The design and transition of services (new or changed) and their requirements should be identified by the customers or stakeholder parties of this service. The Request for Change (RFC) should originate from a business demand or an improvement to the effectiveness of the service. Changes to existing services which could have a major impact on customer or service provider need further risk assessment on whether the change impacts the portfolio or supported business processes. This also applies when services are retired/removed out of the portfolio. Additionally, Service Level contracts are negotiated to offer the necessary and agreed service quality and are changed whenever the relevant service changes.

Service Operation primarily focusses on the operational activities which are needed to maintain and deliver a good service quality for the customer. Therefore it is necessary that operational processes like incident or problem management are not seen as additional costs of the service provided. Management within the Service department and the business itself supports and funds service operation activities. Service operation suffers under the role of daily management business without the prestige of projects initiated in service design or service strategy. Service operation needs to be seen as necessary activity which hast great potential in reducing cost and increasing business value created by the Information services department.

CSI at Merck is carried out as a form of service review and monitoring. Existing SLA's and scopes are regularly reviewed to assess the successful delivery of services to the customer. The service performance is quantified via amount of tickets and availability indicators. Within the SLA's agreed service, availability (Maintenance Windows, Outage handling) and service support (Incident Handling, Service Request Handling) are documented.

3 Management of Risk

3.1 Definition of Risk

According to the ISO Guide 73 for Risk Management, a risk is an effect of uncertainty on objectives. Which directly relies on the business strategy that sets strategic objectives for a measurable business success. Though the effect may be positive, negative or a deviation from the expected it is often described by an event, change in circumstances or a consequence.(ISO, 2009b) As described in chapter 2, alignment between business strategy and IT Strategy is very important for business success. Therefore Risk Management for IT is highly depending on overall enterprise Risk Management principles and processes. The ISACA (Information Systems Audit and Control Association) equals IT risk as a business risk, specifically business risks associated with the use, ownership, operation, involvement, influence and adoption of IT within the enterprise.(ISACA, 2009) This requires risks to be detected or recognized by the businesses even if the majority of them might not have a cost effective factor. It is important that risks resulting from the use of IT are treated as if they have direct impact on the businesses ability to achieve the strategic objectives. Decisions about risk need to be considered so that the potential benefits are worth more than carrying out the risk treatment (OGC, 2010). Risk Management is also increasingly important in conjunction with IT-Governance. Firstly, because the dependence on IT systems and services is growing, on the other hand due to the increasing legal and regulatory requirements (Fröhlich et al., 2007).

3.2 Risk Management principles

Within ISO 31000 several principles for the effective use of Risk Management principles are presented. These act as a guideline for Risk Management to be effective in an organization. Risk Management focusses on the assessment of significant risks and the implementation of suitable responses.(ISO, 2009a)

Therefore Risk Management is a continuous process which aims to support the strategy of the related organization or business. All decisions made by the respective management lead to potential opportunities for benefit, threat to success or an increased degree of uncertainty.

It is important that Risk Management is an integrated part of the businesses' culture which requires commitment towards Risk Management by the executive personnel. Risk objectives must be aligned with strategic and operational objectives, by assigning Risk Management responsibilities throughout the whole organization. In order to successfully adapt to these principles the ISO 31000 defines this structure as Risk Management context (ISO, 2009a).

3.3 Risk Management process

The basic activity advice presented within the ISO 31000 is called the Risk Management process. It should be a part of management activities, embedded into the culture and tailored to the business processes of the respective organization (Hopkin, 2010).

This process describes the activities related to:

- Establishing the above mentioned Risk context

- Risk Assessment (Identification, analysis, evaluation)

- Risk Treatment (toleration, reduction, transfer or termination)

- Related activities such as Risk communication, monitoring

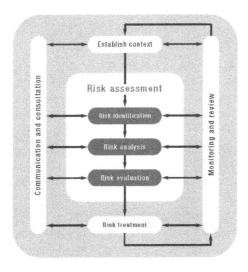

Figure 8 Risk Management Process ISO 31000 (Hopkin, 2010)

Risk Context

When establishing the context, the organization assesses its strategic objectives, defines the involved parameters when managing risk and sets the scope and risk criteria for the process. For the context it is necessary to distinguish between internal and external factors that influence the Risk Management implementation. In IT-Service external influences are the customers / business needs, changes in business strategy or legal, political and financial regulations. For internal purposes the Risk Management process needs to be aligned with the organizations, processes, structure and strategy. For the service providing department (Merck Information Services) this reflects the necessity that Risk Management needs to be a part of every task. When reflecting on objectives and criteria of a particular service/project/process these criteria should always represent the interest of the organization as a whole.(Hopkin, 2010)

Risk Priorities

Defining risk priorities is a crucial process which aims to evaluate the significance of risks. It defines several factors for further risk assessment and treatment. Core objectives are: definition of likelihood, risk level determination, views of stakeholders, the level at which risk becomes tolerable and whether combinations of risks are taken into account.(Hopkin, 2010)

Risk assessment

Starting with risk identification to assess sources of risk, areas of impact, events and their causes and the potential outcomes (positive or negative). This list of risks should state the events that may create, enhance, prevent, degrade, accelerate or delay the achievement of business objectives defined by the organization's strategy. It is important to identify risk even if the source is not able to be influenced by the organization who is facing the risks. To correctly identify risks, personal with appropriate knowledge is essential for this step. Having analyzed the risks the evaluation focusses on the outcomes of risks to determine which of them need to be treated or require a priority treatment. Consequences and likelihood and the level of risk in which they result should reflect the purpose of the risk assessment's output is going to be used. The analysis should be quantitative or qualitative based on the circumstances. To evaluate the risks a comparison between level of risk and risk criteria is established. Based on this a possible approach towards risk treatment can be suggested. Depending on the previously assessed information a decision is to be made if a risk treatment is necessary or if the treatment is going to be worth less than accepting the risk.(Hopkin, 2010)

Risk Treatment

Risk treatment aims to modify the risks so that their outcomes if negative are reduced or a positive aspect can be realized. Based on ISO 31000, several possible treatment options are possible(ISO, 2009a):

- Avoiding the risk by activities that offer the opportunity for risks
- Taking or increasing the risk in order to pursue an opportunity
- Removing the risk source
- Change the likelihood
- Changing the consequences
- Sharing the risk with another party (via contracts)
- Retaining the risk by informed decision

3.4 Risk Management relevant process roles

To address the relevance for the risk assessment and treatment methodologies roles and activities are introduced in this sub chapter: These roles are defined by Merck's Information Service department and relate to proposed roles by the common practice model ITIL in the earlier chapter.

Service Owner:

- Is responsible for service provision, CSI and Service Design
- Develops the service according to business requirements
- Serves as the main contact for representing the provided services to the relationship
- Escalation point in case of major business impacting interruptions
- Manages adequate cost levels in regards of service quality

Relationship Manager:

- Accountable for relationship between Service Provider and customer
- Assures alignment of IT and Business strategy
- Collects SLA requirements for future business demands

- Negotiates on SLA's with customers and manages business expectations
- Performs service reviews with the customer

Service Delivery Manager:

- Accountable for cost efficient delivery of ITSC according to OLA's
- Designs the ITSC in regards of Service Requirements
- Involves SO in issues and escalations
- Coordinates service operation

Risk Manager

- Designs, documents and communicated the Risk Management framework
- Performs regular reviews and updates of the Risk Management framework
- Creates and publishes annual Communication and Consultation Plan
- Provides Risk Assessment methodology
- Maintains Risk Register
- Defines Risk Reporting thresholds
- Performs Risk Reporting
- Provides guidelines on Risk Management procedures

Service Portfolio Manager

- Responsible for creating and reviewing process activities and Standard Operation Procedures (SOPs)
- Ensures implementation and execution of Risk Management activities within the Service Lifecycle
- Responsible for requesting a process audit for the new implemented Risk Management activities for the Service Lifecycle

4   Risk Priorities

In this chapter the Risk Priorities which should be taken into account when assessing risks are identified and discussed. Appropriate Risk Management processes should be followed throughout the life cycle in order to manage identified risk and to determine the rigor and extent of the activities required at each phase of the life cycle.

4.1   Legal and regulatory Risk Priorities

Any deviation of legal or regulatory requirements will lead to risks for an organization. Therefore all of these requirements shall be well known und understood and a regular check of all activities against these requirements are necessary to avoid risks which could harm the organization in a massive way.

As an example for regulatory requirements, this paragraph outlines the 'GxP' regulations. 'GxP' is the generalized term for quality guidelines in regulated industries like food, medical devices, and pharmaceuticals. The aim of these guidelines is to ensure that a product is safe, meets the requirements of the customers and its intended use. As Merck develops and produces life science/health products and pharmaceuticals, the company is subject to these guidelines. Any deviation from these guidelines could lead to the rejection of approval of products by authorities. For all IT-Services which are used in regulated areas there are the GxP requirements of Qualification and Validation.

4.1.1 Qualification

Qualification is hardware and tool based and carries out a qualified hardware configuration and software installation for the respective services and related processes and activities for service operation e.g.:

- Availability Management
- Incident/ Problem management
- Configuration Management
- Change / Release Management
- Disaster Recovery IT-Service Continuity Management

4.1.2 Validation

Validation begins with the configuration and customization of software and application according to business demand. Additionally all GxP relevant services need to be operated by personnel who is regularly trained and qualified according to GxP.

From the Risk Management perspective it is crucial to maintain and validate the quality of the respective service throughout the whole Lifecycle from initiation until a possible retirement of the service. An effective Risk Management approach can ensure a high quality by providing proactive means to identify and control potential issues during development and operations and to avoid any deviations from the regulation requirements. For any service the following questions should be asked to determine the GxP relevance:

- Does the service have an impact on the safety of the patient?

- Does the service have an impact on the product (Quality, Efficacy)?

- Does the system manage critical data for the product?

To assist the analysis, the GAMP (Good automated Manufacturing Practices) Guide was published 2008 in addition to several other guidance documents from the European Union and the FDA. These Guides include but are not limited to the processes and activities that are included in ISO 9000, 20000 and ISO 27001. Additional developed models like RAMP are not taken into account for this procedure (Siconolfi and Bishop, 2007).

Priorities derived from this legal and regulatory influences have an impact on all the phases of a Services' Lifecycle. Activities described as *Qualification* are directly taken from the good practice standard ITIL and its Service Lifecycle phases. The Management of Risk covers a wide angle of activities including BCM, Security, Program/Project and operational Service Management. Merck has decided to address qualification, validation and risk assessment of Services in a general Service Lifecycle procedure as needed.

4.2 Project Initiation Risk Priorities

For each IT-Service requested by the business the initial project requires a BISII (Business IT Strategic Investment Index) analysis to determine its beneficial effect to business value and overall strategic fit. If the proposed service would not fit to either business and/or IT strategy, starting the project could offer substantial risks for the new service or could influence current services in the portfolio in a negative way. As outlined in the previous paragraph, an initial assessment shall also include the determination if the Service will be GxP relevant. This initial assessment should be performed at or before the beginning of the project phase and focus on the determination of the overall impact the service can have on patient safety, product quality and data integrity based on its role for business processes success.(ISPE, 2008) This Assessment should be based on the understanding of business processes and business risk assessments, regulatory and legal requirements and known functional areas. Any relevant previous assessments may provide useful input and these should not be repeated unnecessarily. This risk assessment is likely to focus on important Risks to GxP and on business processes rather than detailed functions or technical aspects (e.g. Change Management or SACM). The process owner and the risk manager are typically involved in addition to appropriate subject matter experts. To successfully perform this first step the following prerequisites should be given:

- A clear understanding of business demand and processes

- Defined boundary around business processes

- The role the service has in supporting the business process

- Sufficiently defined requirements

This initial assessment should offer benefits which lead to the successful implementation of the business supporting IT-Service. By identifying key areas that require focus in various stages of the Lifecycle including KPIs and requirements for developments, service specification and description. Additionally information which assist strategy (business and IT) alignment for achieving the overall objectives of the business. As soon as the scope for the project is set, the information can lead to a successful Service Design phase, developing and providing a service highly aligned with business demand.

4.3 Risk Priorities derived from ITIL

This chapter approaches the analysis of possible risk categories from a bottom-up perspective. ITIL processes which are carried out during the Lifecycle Phases described in chapter 2.2 are reviewed. The ones that are applied and run at Merck' Information Services Department are used to analyze potential risks to be reported for each service and it's responsible Service Owner.

Starting with Service Strategy especially risk associated with the strategic orientation and planning of services and the service organizational structure arise. Covering the whole Service Lifecycle risk may be divided into the following categories which play major or minor roles according to the current Lifecycle phase of the service.

- Service Provider Risks (Service Strategy)
- Contract Risks (Service Design)
- Design Risks (Service Design)
- Operational Risks (Service Operation, Service Transition)

4.3.1 Service Provider Risks

Risk for providers arise when uncertainty originating in the customer's business combines with uncertainty in their operations to have an impact across the service Lifecycle. Risks materialize in various form such as technical problems, loss of control in operations, breaches in information security, delays in launchings services, failure to comply with regulations or lack of financial resources. The exposure to risks and resulting damages are measured in financial terms and in terms of the loss of goodwill among customers, suppliers and partners. While financial losses are undesirable it is at least possible to account for them and write them off against gains elsewhere. It is harder to measure or recover the loss of goodwill in terms of reputation, customer confidence and credibility with prospects. However, financial measures are easier to understand and communicate across organizational boundaries and cultures. To the extent possible it is useful to communicate losses in financial terms, which are then used as indicators rather than direct measures.(OGC, 2011c)

Service provider risks vary by types of providers. The Risk Management plans and budgets of business units may cover Type 1 providers (Internal service provider) such as Merck's Information Services department.

Strategic Management for IT-Services

Responsible executives within the organization are enabled to set objectives for the strategic development of their field of action and to specify how these objectives will be met and where strategic investments are necessary to achieve these objectives. Since the strategy for IT-Services is crucial for delivering a high service quality with an adequate cost structure, this process offers one of the top level risks that determine overall organizations success:

- Insufficient governance controls that allows managers to deviate from overall strategy for short term objectives
- Making strategic decisions when information is missing about internal or external circumstances or using incorrect or misleading information
- Choosing the wrong strategy without proper feedback processes for all related processes which result in the inability to detect and react early on incorrect decisions

Service Portfolio management

Describing the provider's services in terms of business value and articulation of business needs and the clarification of strategic aims is the main focus of running a service portfolio. To achieve this, certain risks should be taken into account:

- Lacking access to business information which leads to insufficient business outcomes and non-existing strategy alignment
- Missing a formal change-, project management or customer- and project portfolio
- Initiating a service without sufficient customer information or enough time to evaluate the service
- Offering a service without proper measurement principles

Demand Management

Seeking to understand, anticipate and influence the customer demand for services and the capacities to meet the business demand is a critical aspect of demand management. Poor management demand is source of risk for service providers which generates cost without any value provided to the customer.

- Lack of accurate configuration management information which leads to estimations about the demand required by the customer
- Service Level management is not able to obtain commitments and is therefore leading to higher levels of investments for the service providers

Business Relationship management (BRM)

BRM enables relationship mangers to provide links between the service provider and the customer at strategic and tactical levels. These links are created to ensure that service providers understand the business requirements and is therefore able to provide services that meet the assessed demand. The main measure whether this purpose is achieved is the level of customer satisfaction.

- Relationship between BRM and other processes can cause confusion about the boundaries and will increase the potential of activities carried out twice
- Disconnections between customer facing processes and more technical focused processes which causes inefficiency of the service provider organization

4.3.2 Contract Risks

Service Design

With every activity within the Service Design Phase of the Service Lifecycle the service provider faces significant challenges which determine the future quality and cost efficiency of the services. Especially when attempting to design new services and processes that meet the business demand and stakeholder requirements. Risks associated with the Design of new services need to be addressed early and in a complete manner to ensure that they won't materialize.

Service Catalogue management

Scope of Service Catalogue Management is to manage the information about currently run services to ensure that they are accurate and reflect current details, status, interfaces and dependencies of all services. Having these information at hand is necessary to prepare for new services being initiated to the live environment.

- Poor access to accurate Change Management Information and processes

- Lack in acceptance of Service Catalogue and its usage for operational processes

- Insufficient tool and resources for maintaining a functional Service Catalogue

Service Level Management

Service Level Management is particularly important to manage the relationship on a contractual basis. Expectations and perceptions of related parties (business and service provider) should be aligned giving a solid bases for an agreed service quality and cost structure. This applies to all currently operated services and planned services in the future. Risk associated with this process offer a significant threat to successful service provision (quality and costs).

- Bypassing the SLM process for faster service deployment

- High customer expectations and low perception

- Poor communication between service provider and business (customer)

- Lacking involvement and commitment from business

Supplier Management

This process ensures that suppliers and the services they provide are managed to support agreed targets and business expectations. It is necessary that supplier management is involved in all stages of the service Lifecycle to support complex business demands which require a broad set of skills and capability. A management of suppliers and their partners is essential to the provision of high quality services towards the business. Supplier Performance according to contracts is one of the main KPIs for Supplier Management.

- Business affected by poor supplier performance

- Compromised service availability

- Unclear ownership of and awareness for contractual issues

- Badly written and agreed contacts that do not support business demand or SLA targets

- Suppliers are not cooperating within the Supplier Management process

- Poor corporate financial processes (procurement and purchasing) prevent a successful Supplier management

4.3.3 Design Risks

Availability Management

Many challenges are concerning Availability Management but the most important one is to meet the agreed expectations of customers. This includes service availability 24 hours, 365 days a year. If they may not, it is regulated that they are recovered based on time frames agreed within the SLAs. Possible risks to meet the Success Factors include the following:

- Missing proactive resource investment to prevent possible failures
- Lack of cooperation between Continuity-, Security and Capacity Management
- Over bureaucratic reporting processes
- Missing service orientation rather than a technological focus

Capacity Management

A major challenge Capacity Management faces is to persuade business to provide information on its strategic plans, enabling the service provider to plan theirs capacities accordingly. To successfully provide services to the business the agreed capacities with in SLAs should be kept. Therefore SLAs have to be created with sufficient information on business demand, to minimize capacity problems for crucial business services. Therefore risks for capacity management include the following aspects:

- Lack of appropriate information from future business plans and strategies
- Lacking alignment between BCM, SCM and CCM
- Reports are too technical and do not give appropriate info to the customers and business

IT-Service Continuity Management

IT-Service continuity is highly depending on an experienced business continuity process. It defines the scope of business services and their demand for supporting IT-Services. Continuity Management must ensure that accurate information is obtained from the BCM process on the needs, impact and priorities of the business. Keeping these to processes aligned is one of the major objective for management of business and IT change organizations. Following risks can interfere with achieving the agreed objectives:

- Insufficient information on business demand

- No conjunction or isolation between related processes (Security- and Availability Management)

- Outdated information about BCM and therefore loss of alignment

Information Security Management

Similar to the alignment necessary for Continuity, IT Security Management cannot be carried out successfully with sufficient business support. Security Controls and assessments are severely limited if they are not able to be enforced throughout the business. The major use of IT-Services and assets is outside of the IT department and so are the majority of security threats and risks. Needs, risks, impacts and priorities for business security management should be aligned and integrated into the ISM process. Therefore risks derived from ISM include the following:

- Unclear policies without integration of business needs

- Ineffective marketing and education in security requirements

- Seeing ITSM as an isolated part from other IT-Service process

With every undertaking there will be challenges or difficulties to face and to overcome. This will be especially true when designing new services and processes that meet business and stakeholder requirements. Understanding business requirements and priorities, communicating with related personnel and function and involving them within the design process is crucial for success.(OGC, 2011a)

4.3.4 Operational Risks

Service Transition

Service Asset and Configuration Management:

SACM is one of the central support Processes facilitating the exchange of information with other processes and as such has few customer facing measures. However, as an underlying engine to other processes in the Lifecycle SACM must be measure for its contribution to these parts of the Lifecycle and the overall KPIs that affect the customer directly (such as Incident- and Problem Management).

Therefore these KPIs can be translated into following risks:

- Incidents or Service failures that are directly related to one particular asset

- Alignment between insurance premiums and business demand

- Insufficient distribution of licenses and underutilization of assets and resources

- Complexity related time increase for diagnosing and resolving incidents

- Unauthorized hardware resulting in long audits as information of the assets is not accessible or non-existent

- Poor Asset data quality and information can result in unauthorized changes

Change Management

While it is relatively easy to count the number of incidents that eventually generate changes, it is infinitely more valuable to look at underlying cause of such changes, and to identify trends. Better still to be able to measure the impact of changes and to demonstrate reduced disruption over time because of implemented Change Management, and to measure the speed and effectiveness with which the service provider responds to identified business demand.

Measures taken should be linked to business goals wherever practical and to cost, service availability and reliability. Therefore risks resulting from process of implementing changes should be assessed.

- High number of unplanned changes (urgent, emergency)

- Disruptions, incidents, problems/errors caused by (unsuccessful) changes and releases

- Frequency of change (by service, business area)

- Low Success rate (percentage of changes deemed successful at review/number of RFCs approved)

Release Management

Release Management aims to build, test and deliver the capability to provide the services specified by Service Design and that will accomplish the stakeholders' requirements and deliver the intended objectives.

- Badly defined scope and understanding of earlier Lifecycle phases which results in a slow and non-measurable release

- Personnel lacking sufficient knowledge, authority and responsibilities to carry out their activities

- Failure of suppliers to meet contractual requirements

- Infrastructure risks (inadequate design, differences/dependencies in infrastructure/applications, Performance failure

The complexity of services across the supply chain is increasing and thus forcing service providers to recognize potential risks to services. Either in transition and as well for releases planned. Close cooperation between support and operations staff is a key success factor for service transition.(OGC, 2011d)

Service Operation

Operational Risks exist throughout different processes located with ITIL Service Operation and Service Transition Phases. Incident Management for example focusses on the documentation and Solving of occurring incidents while operating the Services and Systems. Critical Success factors and KPIs.

Important Risks that should be addressed within this Process and Phase include:

- Lack of available and properly trained resources and personnel
- Unresolved incidents associated with missing information from support tools
- Poorly aligned OLAs and therefore mismatched objectives or actions

Problem Management is highly defendant on a functional Incident Management and its processes and tools. This ensures that problems may be identified as soon as possible. Therefore risk categories that can be derived from Problem Management include the following:

- Poor linking between Incident and Problem Management tools
- Weak relationships between first and second/third level of support
- Missing understanding of business impact by problem management staff

Ultimately the greatest risk of all for the service operation phase is the loss of functionality of a specific service and therefore impact on employees, customers and finances (OGC, 2011b). In extreme cases such as GxP regulated Systems and services a risk for health or safety of patients is imminent. One of the most critical Risk is the Lack of Management support for Operational Processes and the Loss of key personnel.

5 Risk Management Methods

While risk-based decision making should be used throughout the life cycle, different approaches may be appropriate to different situations, ranging from formal risk assessment to decision taking into account pertinent risk factors.

5.1 Determination of Risk Priorities

In order to effectively apply a Risk Management program to provided services and systems it is important to have thorough understanding of the business processes which are supported by the services. This includes in terms of pharmaceutical business impact on patient safety, product quality and data integrity. ICH Guideline defines hazards, harms and impacts of risks for every service currently operated. (ICH, 2005) Defines Harm as Damage to health, including the damage that can occur from loss of product quality or availability, whereas hazard is the source of harm. Together with the severity, which measures the possible outcomes of a hazard the definition leads to the risk. A combination of probability of occurrence including harm and its severity.

To determine the relevance of risks and therefore managing the resources associated with Risk Management, risks need to be prioritized according to their impact on business processes. Introducing a risk classification from a combined factor probability and severity will give a first impression how critical the risks are. The prioritization takes this risk class and sets a detectability factor which defines the likelihood that the fault in the service or systems will be detected before the harm can occur.

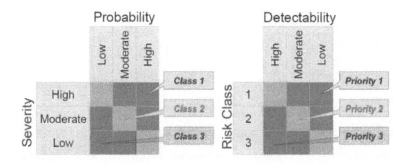

Figure 9 Risk prioritization(ISPE, 2008)

5.2   Risk Tolerance for IT-Services

Based on applicability of GxP regulations or regulations concerning electronic records(FDA, 2007) the use of Information Services for pharmaceutical research and production processes demand a strict procedure to cover the risks. Very few to zero tolerance is given from the institution if the agreed standards are not met. A prohibition of production or distribution of pharmaceutical products is one of the greatest risks a company such as Merck can face. Therefore risks posed to violate the agreed standards should receive not tolerance when determining the priorities of risks. Secondly *patient and product safety* as well as *record integrity* should not be given any tolerance when treating associated risks.

The Risk Priority Factor achieved in the previous sub chapter is highly dependable on:

- Types of data the service or system handles

- Types of functions it performs

- Likeliness of exposure to user actions that may identify system errors and trigger systems correction and maintenance

Every area can be rated by a risk level which indicates the level of susceptibility is existing towards patient and product safety and record integrity. Based on this indication, recommendation can be made which amount of risk is tolerable for certain processes and functions. (ISPE, 2008)

5.3   Risk Review Checkpoints

To give the responsible service owner the ability to assess risks associated with his service, certain checkpoints during the Lifecycle are pointed out. Like mentioned before, the services run through multiple phases which are defined by ITIL and supported by their respective processes. The service Owner is enabled to get input from the responsible process owner for the specific process.

5.3.1 Phase Transitions

Figure 10 Phase Transition Risk Review

If services are operated and therefore change from Initiation and preparation towards operation this certain event should be chosen to assess the current risk posed to the risk itself and other services which are depending on the service or are influenced by its output. These transitions are possible in three different ways:

- Initiation → preparation

- Preparation → operation

- Operation → retirement

5.3.2 Major Events (Releases, Changes and Incidents)

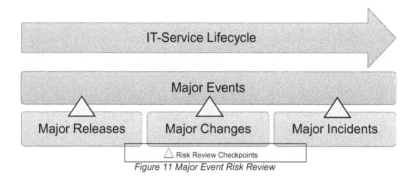
Figure 11 Major Event Risk Review

Since the quality and cost structure of the service is highly dependable on an proactive change- , incident- and release management major events in this categories should be used for and additional risk assessment. This direct serves the overall service quality, reducing possible impacts on other services and systems. To achieve the best output from this risk checkpoint all ITIL processes that give info on the current state of the service should be consulted at this point.

For example a close cooperation of the operational processes (incident- and problem management) and SACM is crucial for valid and correct information on the service. Additionally a history of Incident or change records could serve this purpose as well.

5.3.3 Regular Risk Assessment

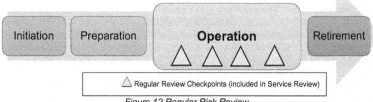

Figure 12 Regular Risk Review

A service review process is carried out every year to determine its quality defined by customer satisfaction, costs and SLA related data such as availability and capacity planning. During this review several processes can give significant input to further enhance the service quality, costs and performance. This can be done in a small scope based on operational KPIs such as amount of service related incidents or unsuccessful changes. If the service review with the included risk determination shall be executed for the best possible outcome additional activities relating to earlier Lifecycle phases should be taken into account. Demand Management for example gives significant input on customer requirements and business objectives which directly links to capacities managed that should be met by service provided. Simple SLA fulfillment by the service provider won't indicate if the service is provided under mutual beneficial circumstances for customer and provider.

5.3.4 Legal or regulatory Changes

If not covered by the previously described service review, changes in legal or regulatory requirements need to be treated according to their criticality and impact on business. Meaning if the FDA initiates a new standard on how computerized productions systems need to be managed. But the current supporting services at Merck do not meet this standard they pose a significant risk for achieving overall business objectives. Therefore the service owner is responsible to get information on changes that could affect the services in his responsibility from following organizations:

- Corporate Quality assurance

- Corporate Governance

- IT-Governance

Usually these are not overnight changes and affected companies such as Merck have to react accordingly. Changes to Productions standards are usually proposed in several versions until they fully apply by legislative decisions. Therefore this process takes several month or even years until a new standards is published. Given this procedure required actions by the service owner will only need to be carried out in special circumstances and not regularly.

5.4   Risk Priority Checkpoints

In Chapter 4.3 risk priorities were assessed through ITIL processes and by their respective owners at Merck. These risk priorities are now used to create distinguished recommendations on how and which risks need to be taken into account at the specific checkpoints. Furthermore the related processes which are related to the risks are identified. The Service Owner can now evaluate the risks and decide in which case more input or more detailed information is needed and who is responsible to provide the needed information.

5.4.1 Phase Transitions:

Initiation → preparation:

If the service has proved a value to the business from previous assessment with the BISII procedure its status is changed from Initiation to Preparation.

Risk Priority	Related ITIL Process Input
Incomplete understanding of business demand	Strategic MGMT for Services
Unclear defined requirements	Strategic MGMT for Services
Missing strategic alignment of Services	Strategic MGMT for Services
Lack of access to business information	Service Portfolio MGMT
Missing evaluation of Service	Service Portfolio MGMT
Missing customer portfolio	Service Portfolio MGMT
Missing Service Level Commitment from Customer	Demand MGMT
Missing technical Info	Business Relationship MGMT

Table 2 Risk Priorities Phase Transition: Initiation → Preparation

Preparation → Operation

Given the situation that all of the previously planned and designed aspects of the new service are now put into operational environment, various risks need to be taken into account with this phase. It is very important to include experiences which were learned when setting up services in the past. This will help when taking certain decisions. Information which support the process of running an IT-Service come from various processes and persons. Technical as well as contractual and regulatory information need to be clarified beforehand to guarantee a smooth transition into operational environment.

Risk Priority	Related ITIL Process Input
Inaccurate Change Management Info	Change MGMT
Insufficient Tools and resources	SACM
High customer expectations	Service Level MGMT
Lack of communication between provider and business	Business Relationship MGMT
Missing commitment and involvement of business	Service Level MGMT
Bypassing the SLA process for faster service deployment	Service Level MGMT
Poor supplier performance	Supplier MGMT
Unclear ownership for contractual issues	Supplier MGMT
Bad Contracts that don't support SLA or business success	Supplier MGMT
Poor corporate processes (Procurement) inhibit the success of supplier MGMT	Supplier MGMT
Missing proactive resources to prevent failures	Availability MGMT
Lack of cooperation between related processes	Availability-, Capacity-, Continuity-MGMT
Over bureaucratic reporting	Availability MGMT
Lack of appropriate information form business plans and strategies	Capacity-, Continuity MGMT
Lack of Alignment between BCM, SCM and CCM	Capacity MGMT

Insufficient Info from reports for the customers	Capacity MGMT
Overall too technical focus	Availability-, Capacity-, Continuity MGMT
Unclear policies without commitment from the business	IT Security MGMT
Ineffective Education in security requirements	IT Security MGMT
Lack of integration to all IT related processes	IT Security MGMT
Lack of operational information on adequate service levels	Incident MGMT

Table 3 Risk Priorities Phase Transition Preparation → Operation

Operation → Retirement

When talking about system or service retirement a differentiation of different processes should be established. If the Service is removed from active operation when for example users are deactivated or interfaces are disabled. No data should be added to the Service after this point. Special access should be retained for data reporting or results analysis and general support. In the case of service disposal, software and related hardware will be permanently removed. Each service should reach this stage at a different time. Data and documentation should not be disposed until they have reached the end of their record retention period, as specified in the related policies. Due to the amount of data and the scale of the related information systems the disposal of a service will be a major task. Consideration should be given to the following risks:

Risk Priority	Related ITIL Process Input
Missing documentation of actions during retirement (migration, removal of data)	Change MGMT
Lack of business related info	Business Relationship MGMT
Lack of information to business about changes to business processes	Business Relationship MGMT
Lack of cooperation between related processes	Availability-, Capacity-, Continuity-MGMT
Lack of sufficient Continuity plans	Continuity MGMT
Missing decisions on data retention aligned with business objectives	Demand MGMT
Incorrect documentation of service retirement	Service Catalogue MGMT
Discontinuing of related Service Level Contracts	Service Level MGMT
Missing technical Info from former Incidents or Problems	Incident Problem MGMT

Table 4 Risk Priorities Phase Transition Operation → Retirement

5.4.2 Major Events (Releases, Changes and Incidents)

Major Releases

Planning for major releases of Services such as version or functionality upgrades needs to be carefully planned. Usually if the release is of significant impact according to resources (finances, staff and technology) a dedicated project will be initiated. Otherwise if the change serves purposes of improvement in service quality and costs, the release will be scheduled within a regular release and deployment plan.

This process is relying on different input from various supporting Phases such as Service Design and Service Operation. Therefore risks associated with previous Lifecycle Stages are also taken into account:

Risk Priority	Related ITIL Process Input
Poorly defined Scope and understanding of previous Lifecycle stages	Processes of Service Design
Staff is not committed to release	Release MGMT
Financial insufficiencies	Strategic MGMT for IT-Services
Missing Controls (policies, security, software licensing)	IT Security-, Continuity, MGMT
Unexpected changes in regulatory controls or requirements	Business Relationship MGMT
Unclear expectations/objectives of customers, suppliers and users	Demand MGMT
Indecision or Late decision making	Release MGMT
Insufficient Time allowed for the release	Release MGMT
Failure to meet contractual agreements (suppliers and business)	Service Level-, Supplier-, Demand- MGMT
Differences/Independencies in Infrastructure/Applications	SACM

Table 5 Risk Priorities Major Releases

Major Changes

Changes to IT-Services are made for a variety of reasons these could include:

- Proactive changes to seek business benefits such as reduction in cost, improved services, increased effectives of support

- Reactively to resolve errors and adapting to changing circumstances

It is therefore necessary to assess and prioritize the risks which are associated with the change. Being able to determine the overall impact on business and provider the change of the service could give a significant better opportunity to plan the change process accordingly. For this change management process applicable risks should be asses beforehand.

Risk Priority	Related ITIL Process Input
Lack of commitment and sponsorship to the change management process by business	Business Relationship MGMT
Insufficient time and resource allowance for assessment of changes	Change MGMT
Lack of process cooperation form Service Design and Service Operation	Strategic MGMT for IT-Services
Excessively bureaucratic change management process	Change MGMT
Insufficient information on underlying technology	SACM
High Number of unplanned changes	Change MGMT

Table 6 Risk Priorities Major Changes

Major Incidents

Major Outages or unplanned service interruptions need to be treated and resolved as soon as possible to reduce the business process downtime and therefore higher levels of availability. Given the ITIL definition of Incident a reduction in service quality or a failure of certain service components, can cause this outages. Usually Major incidents are routed towards problem management to assure that interruptions of this kind do not occur again. Root cause analysis is carried out to determine the source of failure whether it is a service component or human error. It is necessary that former incidents and problems are documented within the supporting tools to offer a better information support to staff that is responsible reacting to such major outages. Therefore risk associated with the resolving of incidents should include the following ones.

Risk Priority	Related ITIL Process Input
Inadequate capacities or planned availability	Availability- and Capacity MGMT
Insufficient incident matching procedure	Incident- and Problem MGMT
Lack of process cooperation form Service Design and Service Operation	Strategic MGMT for IT-Services
Lack of correct incident prioritization	Change MGMT
Insufficient information on underlying technology	SACM
Insufficient Logging of Incidents	Incident MGMT
High backlog of Incident for services	Incident MGMT
Total number of Incidents and Problems per Service	Incident- and Problem MGMT
Poorly aligned OLAs	Incident- and Problem MGMT

Table 7 Risk Priorities Major Incidents

5.4.3 Regular Service Review

For every IT-Service run in Merck's Service Portfolio a mandatory yearly service review is carried out. This includes common activities such as review of agreed Service Level contracts therefore planned capacities and agreed availability plans that are delivered for the business and customer. Related stakeholders from business, relationship manger and service owner take part within this process. The review primarily focusses on service quality, performance and costs.

CORPORATE SERVICE LEVELS		Bronze	Silver	Gold
Service Availability		24 hrs x 7 days	24 hrs x 7 days	24 hrs x 7 days
Maintenance Windows (frame for planned Service unavailability) Timezone CET if not changed in SLA		**1 week** notice Mon-Thu 18:00 - 08:00 Fri 18:00 - Mon 08:00	**2 weeks** notice Mon-Thu 18:00 - 08:00 Fri 18:00 - Mon 08:00 *other timeframe optional*	**4 weeks** notice Mon-Fri *none* Sat 08:00 - Sun 23:00 *other timeframe optional*
Outage Handling (max. outage time per reporting period during indicated time frame)		Max. **24 hours** per month (24h x 5d, Mon - Fri) *Availability appr. 95 %*	Max. **16 hours** per month (24h x 5d, Mon - Fri) *Availability appr. 97 %*	Max. **4 hours** per month (24h x 7d, Mon - Sun) *Availability appr. 99,5 %*
Disaster Recovery		undefined (> 30 days)	< 20 days	< 4 hours
Service Desk / 1st Level Support		24 hrs x 7 days	24 hrs x 7 days	24 hrs x 7 days
Application Support (2nd & 3rd Level) Timezone CET if not changed in SLA		**8 hrs x 5 days** *9:00 - 17:00, Mon - Fri*	**10 hrs x 5 days** *8:00 - 18:00, Mon - Fri extra hours optional*	**10 hrs x 5 days** *8:00 - 18:00, Mon - Fri extra hours optional*
Incident Handling (Mon-Fri)				
Incident Priority (90% resolved in …)		n/a	1,5 days	1 day
Incident Standard (90% resolved in …)		3 days	2,5 days	2 days
Service Request Handling (Mon-Fri)				
Service Request Priority (90% resolved in …)		1 day	0,5 days	0,3 days
Service Request Standard (90% resolved in …)		3 days	2,5 days	2 days

Figure 13 Corporate Merck Service Levels (Merck 2013)

Planned changes as well as feedback from the business are collected to determine the alignment with business demand and objectives. Additionally supplier quality, control of changes (completeness and accuracy) and applicability of regulatory requirements is reviewed. The review results are classified according to KIPs shown below.

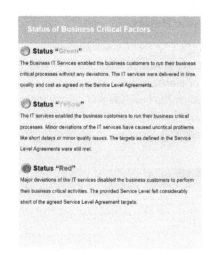

Figure 14 Status of Reviewed Services (Merck 2013)

In the best case the IT-Service is reviewed with a status "Green" which indicates the best possible support for business processes and their objectives. The remaining status are significantly worse for business performance and therefore require additional review of factors which resulted in the bad service performance.

This review process should now be enhanced with a regular Risk Management perspective, which gives information on current risk classification, priority. This methodology further supports the decision making process and determination if the reviewed service poses a risk to overall business objectives, other services within the portfolio and or strategic decision of the IT-Services department. This Risk Management methodology is carried out in addition to the risk priorities covered at major events in the service Lifecycle described in chapter 5.4.2. This Risk Management approach includes but is not limited to the following risk priorities:

Risk Priority	Related ITIL Process Input
Inadequate capacities or planned availability	Availability- and Capacity MGMT
Insufficient incident matching procedure	Incident- and Problem MGMT
Lack of process cooperation form Service Design and Service Operation	Strategic MGMT for IT-Services
Insufficient information on underlying technology	SACM
Insufficient Logging of Incidents	Incident MGMT
Total number of Incidents and Problems per Service	Incident- and Problem MGMT
Poorly aligned OLAs	Incident- and Problem MGMT
Technical independencies of services	SACM
High customer expectations	Service Level MGMT
Access to business information	Service Portfolio MGMT
Missing Service Level Commitment from Customer	Demand MGMT
Missing proactive resources to prevent failures	Availability MGMT
Lack of cooperation between related processes	Availability-, Capacity-, Continuity- MGMT
Lack of appropriate information form business plans and strategies	Capacity-, Continuity MGMT
Unclear policies without commitment from the business	IT Security MGMT
Ineffective Education in security requirements	IT Security MGMT

Table 8 Risk Priorities Regular Service Review

5.4.4 Legal or regulatory Changes

To assist the process of regulatory compliance, verification and qualification of services and personnel the previously described service review should be extended to serve this purpose. Services and Systems that are applicable to regulatory requirements from institutions such as the FDA should be kept under a strict quality assurance based on GxP standards. This even applies to related third party suppliers and business stakeholders.

To secure the compliance to given requirements several standards procedures should be applied. These include but are not limited to:

- Service and System Documentation Status (verification and Qualification)

- Current and New Supplier Qualification

- Change Effectiveness, Success and Completeness

- Applicability of regulatory Frameworks and requirements

- Legal regulations for data privacy and personal information

Therefore associated risks priorities should be assessed:

Risk Priority	Related ITIL Process Input
Lack of commitment and sponsorship to the change management process by business	Business Relationship MGMT
Insufficient time and resource allowance for assessment of changes	Change MGMT
Lack of process cooperation form Service Design and Service Operation	Strategic MGMT for IT-Services
Excessively bureaucratic change management process	Change MGMT
Insufficient information on underlying technology	SACM
High Number of unplanned changes	Change MGMT

Table 9 Risk Priorities legal and regulatory Changes

6   Management of Risk Priority Checkpoints

The aim of managing risks is to achieve lower costs by anticipating and managing a potential risk rather than to recover from an issue that is affecting the achievement of strategic or operational objectives. Fitting the risk context and engaging stakeholder into the process of respective organization further increases the importance which the management of risk should have in an overall business and IT perspective.

It should provide clear guidance, inform decision making and create a supportive culture to achieve measurable value for the organization. (OGC, 2010) Based on an agreed Risk Management Policy the procedure of applying risks to the Lifecycle of an IT-Service should be determined by the phase of the Service.

Decisions at the beginning of the Lifecycle (Initiation and Preparation Phase) should be covered by a long-term view on strategic objectives and their associated risks which could hinder the successful provision of future services. During the Operation Phase emphasis should be put on short term objectives and risk they are confronted with. Which doesn't mean that information included in these two approaches should not be exchanged. All risk exposures which an organizations faces should be able to addressed accordingly. The flow of information on risk should not end with the field of responsibility in one department since the risk identified could have serious impact on how another department handles their operational processes and functions.

The twist is not slavishly and prudently avoiding, reducing, transferring or accepting risk, but to consciously balance the value the enterprise is prepared to actively put at risk in order to obtain the benefits of the opportunity. In addition, they actively assess the scale of exposure that is tolerable and justifiable should the risk be realized.(Drew, 2007) Additionally, potential future issues or risks should be monitored and documented. A possible approach is presented through term of *Horizon Scanning(Drew, 2007)*.

This chapter is focused on the previously described Risk Management principles and process. These are used to point out activities which should be carried out to initiate a more efficient Risk Management approach for the complete Lifecycle of an IT-Service.

6.1 Risk Treatment

As described in chapter 3 the introduced Risk Management process derived from ISO 31000 is executed in accordance to corporate standards. The decision taking on how risks are treated is highly dependable on the extent to which the risk is applicable to the current state the IT-Service resides in.

Risk Toleration

Specifically pointed out in the previous chapter 5.2 services and systems that directly support regulated laboratory, clinical and manufacturing processes are subject to very strict regulations. Therefore a low to zero risk tolerance is advised. Opportunities which could be pursued by tolerating and accepting the risks are close to non-existence. The negative effects on the ability to achieve business objectives is overweighing to such an extent that this procedure is *not acceptable.*

Risk Reduction

Generally speaking the procedure of risk reduction focusses on not pursuing an opportunity or just refrain the risk related activity. Based on the context and the specific checkpoint at which the risk is determined the procedure of risk reduction will differ in which way the risks are reduced. Given the situation that the risk is information or communication based. Interfaces between processes that are based on each other's information input and output these interfaces need to be enhanced and supported by management decisions to be prosperous in the future.

Risk Transfer

Risk that can be treated by setting up contracts or insuring against possible service interruptions are the proposed procedure when taking transfer of risks into account. Even though contracts between service provider, third party supplier or customers should be mutual beneficial they also serve the purpose of insuring against contractual failures of any participating organization. Insuring against possible risk related failures is only achievable if the regularly paid premiums don't exceed amount that are appropriate to the service insured.

Selecting the most appropriate risk treatment option involves balancing the costs and efforts of implementations against the benefits derived, with regards to legal, regulatory and other requirements such as social responsibility and the protection against natural environment.(ISO, 2009a) Additional proposed treatment options like Risk financing (Borgehesi and Gaudenzi, 2013) where taken into account but will not be applicable to Merck's corporate needs.

6.2 Risk Communication

Sharing information about risk and Risk Management between decision makers (risk manager and service owner) should be a common practice. The output of the Risk Management process, including the assessments of impact and risk and the evaluated effectiveness of monitored controls should be accessible by other involved parties (relationship manager, service delivery manager and service portfolio manager). The communication should take place throughout the Risk Management process. Although not necessary to communicate every assessment or treatment of risk special emphasis should be given when a risk or impact changes, so that any necessary adjustment can be made. When necessary the process should enable escalation of risks to senior managers in a timely fashion.

Risk communication may be a part of a wider communications plan for the activity in question, or a specific risk communications plan may be created. Effective communication between stakeholders is a critical success factor for Risk Management, to ensure that context is understood, risks are identified and assed, and suitable responses planned and owned. As with all communication plans two-way communication is essential so the plan must outline processes for handling feedback as well as information about messages to be transmitted.(OGC, 2010)

The information can also be used to improve the efficiency of the change management process. Every change to be applied can use the risk assessment information to identify the areas of the service or process impacted by the change and the risk by executing the change. To facilitate this communication, risk assessment should be documented so that the results can be easily accessed during the life cycle. This may be achieved by using a risk register specific for each service. This risk register should be available to all decision making parties involved such as Service owner and risk manager. This approach will be effective if the risk control strategies that are put in place are monitored during the life of the service to ensure they remain in place and are effective. Hence previously documented control strategies can be adapted to similar services in the future. As part of the periodic review the risk register should be reviewed to ensure that all controls and strategies remain appropriate.

7   Visualization for Service Review

To assist the process of risk assessment, evaluation and management a portfolio visualization of the regular service review risk priorities is proposed. This aims to give appropriate means to demonstrate and compare the risk levels (impact * likelihood) of the reviewed services. The responsible service owner is enabled to see the overall risk level for the respective service and comparisons to previous risk reviews.

The Risk Level are interpreted as shown follows with information on the overall risk levels

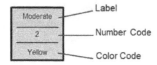

The matrix below shows the classification of risk levels according to likelihood and impact. Necessary information on risk prioritization are created beforehand and need as input for this matrix. The risk priority acquisition is described in the previous chapter 5.4.

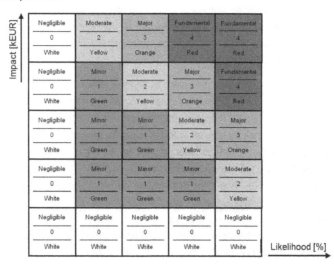

Figure 15 Risk Level Matrix (Merck 2013)

Aiming for a better decision making assistance this risk level overview is used to provide information resulting out of service review check points. The Service Owner gains the ability to check the risk level history and development of his service several years retrospectively. Offering information on former treatment solutions for risks and their sources can be accessed and used to determine and evaluate the current situation of the respective service. A possible visualization in two different levels is proposed below:

SERVICE ID:	XYZ123				
RISK CHECKPOINTS	CP 1	CP 2	CP 3	CP 4	CP 5
Date	dd.mm.yy	dd.mm.yy	dd.mm.yy	dd.mm.yy	dd.mm.yy
RISK LEVEL	4	3	2	1	0
Service Details #1					
Service Details #2					
Service Details #3					
Service Details #4					
Service Details #5					

Table 10 Risk Level Visualization for IT-Services

The second table below gives a more detailed on the specific risks which determine the overall risk level for the Service. The primary source of the risk level is shown, which gives an important overview on the exact status of the Service and its associated risks. As an example high priority risks with *Risk Level 4* were chosen pointing out at which checkpoint risks of that level where assessed and how they were treated.

SERVICE ID:	XYZ123				
RISK LEVEL	4				
RISK CHECKPOINTS	CP 1	CP 2	CP 3	CP 4	CP 5
Date	dd.mm.yy	dd.mm.yy	dd.mm.yy	dd.mm.yy	dd.mm.yy
Risk Details#1					
Risk Details#2					
Risk Details#3					
Risk Details#4					
Risk Details#5					

Table 11 Risk Level Details at specific checkpoints

8   Results

The key to success of the presented methodology lies in its simplicity. By adopting various standards for the provision of IT-Services such as ITIL, organizations face various opportunities but also risks when adhering to these standards. Often specific processes and functions are presented as a guarantee to better service quality, higher customer satisfaction and cost reduction. But this might not always be true. The implementation of certain processes is highly complex and cost intensive so that the decision on implementation has to be in accordance with the strategic objectives. Problems with implementing standards occur when personnel do not adhere to these standards or lack the perception of the overall strategic objectives.

This efficient method proved to be suitable by improving information exchange between related processes. Even though the information output (e.g. number of incidents per time frame for a specific service) was always readily available, this exchange was never applied to Risk Management.

Thus the presented methodology is far easier to apply than previously assumed. Whether or not minor changes to existing processes have to be made, the expected outcome and support towards short or long-term decision making will prove its worth.

As the Risk Management process is already a well-known and widely applied approach the additionally obtained service specific information further improves its support for business success.

9 Conclusion

Though not widely accepted as a necessity for good management and therefore a foundation for strategic (long-term) or operational (short-term) decisions Risk Management in IT-Service Management proves its worth. Taking risks and possibly not being able to provide the agreed services, the so-called service-loss, is one thing which should not occur under any circumstances.

This Thesis *Risk Management within the IT-Service Lifecycle* set out to provide a methodology on which these long and short term decisions should be based and therefore strengthen the basis of any management action. The study sought to find applied standards, processes and principles that could offer such a methodology without implementing additional principles.

The general theoretical literature on this subject and specifically in the context of strategy and operation were based on the *de facto* standard for IT-Service Organizations *ITIL* and common Risk Management methods *ISO 31000*. Background knowledge on how the service Industry developed are presented for understanding purposes. These applied standards sought to answer the following question:

1. When should IT-Service organization assess the risks for their provided services?

2. On which informational input should these assessments be based?

The concept of using already available information from applied ITIL processes and organizational structures has proved to be applicable for the given situation at Merck. Management of Risk (OGC, 2010) has proved to be a good recommendation on which future implementations could be based. For future purposes in cases of practicable implementations different standards and models will offer additional input on this methodology. These include COBIT, ISO/IEC 21000, GAMP and Six Sigma. As these management practices are already implemented at Merck, the methodology can easily be expanded to serve the purpose.

As Risk Management should be an integral part of the Management of IT-Services and their organizations, a lot research can still be done within this field. Often Risk Management for IT-Services is only focused on the risks posed by IT-Security Issues. This Thesis shows that a lot of different processes and functions from IT organizations pose risks towards the service provisions as well to the business itself. In cases of Service Lifecycle Management the article (Fischbach et al., 2013) presented two different trends: an IT-oriented and business-oriented approach towards the management of services and their production. There is a high possibility that these two approaches will converge into a new way of designing, developing and operating services in the future.

This Thesis has offered an evaluative perspective on an important aspect of implementing Risk Management into the management of services within their lifecycle. As a direct consequence the approach was limited to ITIL. As far as ITIL goes it has proven to be worthwhile making decisions based on internal information. To extend the applicability and even test the methodology for a broader scope and angle, other standards can be used to compare and evaluate the information obtained from ITIL.

Although Risk Management is often seen as a methodology solely for senior executives, they also have to establish a common sense and a culture for risk throughout their whole organization.

In spite of what is often reported about the implementation of Risk Management, Senior Executives have to establish a common sense and culture for Risk. Not only are risks easier to treat if they are recognized and communicated accordingly, but all employees within a company can also improve their own approaches towards making decisions, whether they are large or small.

List of References

BEIMS, M. 2012. *IT-Service Management in der Praxis mit ITIL® ITIL® Edition 2011, ISO 20000:2011 und Prince2® in der Praxis,* München, Hanser.

BORGEHESI, A. & GAUDENZI, B. 2013. *Risk Management,* Milano, Springer Milan.

BULLINGER, H. J., SCHEER, A.-W. & SCHNEIDER, K. 2006. *Service Engineering Entwicklung und Gestaltung innovativer Dienstleistungen,* Berlin, Springer.

DEMING, E. 1986. *Out of the Crisis,* McGraw-Hill Inc.

DREW, M. 2007. Information risk management and compliance—expect the unexpected. *BT Technology Journal,* 25, 19-29.

EREK, K. 2012. *Nachhaltiges Informationsmanagement: Gestaltungsansätze und Handlungsempfehlungen für IT-Organisationen.* Univ.-Verl. der TU.

FDA 2007. Guidance for Industry Computerized Systems Used in Clinical Investigations. Department of Health and Human Services.

FISCHBACH, M., PUSCHMANN, T. & ALT, R. 2013. Service Lifecycle Management. *Business & Information Systems Engineering,* 5, 45-49.

FRÖHLICH, M., GLASNER, K., GOEKEN, M. & JOHANNSEN, W. 2007. Sichten der IT Governance. *Governance,* 3-8.

HOPKIN, P. 2010. *Fundamentals of risk management understanding, evaluating, and implementing effective risk management,* London; Philadelphia, PA, Kogan Page.

ICH 2005. Q9 Tripartite Guideline Quality Risk Management. *International Conference on Harmonization of technical requirements for registration of pharmaceuticals for Human use.* ICH Steering Commitee.

ISACA 2009. *The risk IT framework principles, process details, management guidelines, maturity models,* Rolling Meadows, IL, ISACA.

ISO 2009a. ISO 31000. Geneva: ISO Copiright Office.

ISO 2009b. ISO Guide 73:2009. Geneva: ISO Copiright Office.

ISO 2012. ISO/IEC 20000-2, Information Technology - Service management. *Part2: Guidance on application of service management systems.* Geneva: ISO Copiright Office.

ISPE 2008. *GAMP 5 - A Risk-Based Approach to Compliant GxP Computerized Systems.*

MATYS, E. 2013. *Praxishandbuch Produktmanagement: Grundlagen und Instrumente,* Frankfurt am Main, Campus.

OGC 2010. *Management of Risk: Guidance for Practioners,* London, The Stationary Office.

OGC 2011a. *ITIL Service Design,* London, The Stationery Office.

OGC 2011b. *ITIL Service Operation,* London, The Stationary Office.

OGC 2011c. *ITIL Service Strategy,* London, The Stationary Office.

OGC 2011d. *ITIL Service Transition,* London, The Stationary Office.

PORTER, M. 1980. Competitive Strategy: Techniques for Analyzing Industries and Competitors. *The Free Press.*

SICONOLFI, R. M. & BISHOP, S. 2007. RAMP (risk assessment and management process): an approach to risk-based computer system validation and Part 11 compliance. *Drug information journal,* 41, 69-79.

WOITSCH, R., KARAGIANNIS, D., PLEXOUSAKIS, D. & HINKELMANN, K. 2009. Business and IT alignment: the IT-Socket. *e & i Elektrotechnik und Informationstechnik,* 126, 308-321.

ZARNEKOW, R. & BRENNER, W. 2003. Auf dem Weg zu einem produkt-und dienstleistungsorientierten IT-Management. *HMD-Praxis der Wirtschaftsinformatik,* 40, 7-16.

ZARNEKOW, R., BRENNER, W. & PILGRAM, U. 2003. *Integriertes Informationsmanagement,* Berlin [u.a.], Springer.

ZIMIN, V. V. & KULAKOV, S. M. 2010. Dynamic lifecycle management of IT services in corporate information systems. *Steel in Translation,* 40, 539-548.